Monthly Planner

Month: ____________ **Year:** ____________

Monday	Tuesday	Wednesday	Thursday	Friday	Saturday	Sunday

Notes:

Monthly Planner

Month: ________ **Year:** ________

Monday	Tuesday	Wednesday	Thursday	Friday	Saturday	Sunday

Notes:

Monthly Planner

Month: ________ **Year:** ________

Monday	Tuesday	Wednesday	Thursday	Friday	Saturday	Sunday

Notes:

Monthly Planner

Month: ________ **Year:** ________

Monday	Tuesday	Wednesday	Thursday	Friday	Saturday	Sunday

Notes:

Monthly Planner

Month: ________ **Year:** ________

Monday	Tuesday	Wednesday	Thursday	Friday	Saturday	Sunday

Notes:

Monthly Planner

Month: ________ **Year:** ________

Monday	Tuesday	Wednesday	Thursday	Friday	Saturday	Sunday

Notes:

Monthly Planner

Month: ____________ **Year:** ____________

Monday	Tuesday	Wednesday	Thursday	Friday	Saturday	Sunday

Notes:

Monthly Planner

Month: ________ **Year:** ________

Monday	Tuesday	Wednesday	Thursday	Friday	Saturday	Sunday

Notes:

Monthly Planner

Month: ________ **Year:** ________

Monday	Tuesday	Wednesday	Thursday	Friday	Saturday	Sunday

Notes:

Monthly Planner

Month: ________ **Year:** ________

Monday	Tuesday	Wednesday	Thursday	Friday	Saturday	Sunday

Notes:

Monthly Planner

Month: ________ **Year:** ________

Monday	Tuesday	Wednesday	Thursday	Friday	Saturday	Sunday

Notes:

Monthly Planner

Month: __________ **Year:** __________

Monday	Tuesday	Wednesday	Thursday	Friday	Saturday	Sunday

Notes:

Monthly Planner

Month: ________ **Year:** ________

Monday	Tuesday	Wednesday	Thursday	Friday	Saturday	Sunday

Notes:

Monthly Planner

Month: ________ **Year:** ________

Monday	Tuesday	Wednesday	Thursday	Friday	Saturday	Sunday

Notes:

Monthly Planner

Month: ________ **Year:** ________

Monday	Tuesday	Wednesday	Thursday	Friday	Saturday	Sunday
☐	☐	☐	☐	☐	☐	☐
☐	☐	☐	☐	☐	☐	☐
☐	☐	☐	☐	☐	☐	☐
☐	☐	☐	☐	☐	☐	☐
☐	☐	☐	☐	☐	☐	☐

Notes:

Monthly Planner

Month: ________ **Year:** ________

Monday	Tuesday	Wednesday	Thursday	Friday	Saturday	Sunday

Notes:

Monthly Planner

Month: ________ **Year:** ________

Monday	Tuesday	Wednesday	Thursday	Friday	Saturday	Sunday

Notes:

Monthly Planner

Month: ________ **Year:** ________

Monday	Tuesday	Wednesday	Thursday	Friday	Saturday	Sunday

Notes:

Monthly Planner

Month: ________ **Year:** ________

Monday	Tuesday	Wednesday	Thursday	Friday	Saturday	Sunday

Notes:

Monthly Planner

Month: ________ Year: ________

Monday	Tuesday	Wednesday	Thursday	Friday	Saturday	Sunday

Notes:

Monthly Planner

Month: ________ Year: ________

Monday	Tuesday	Wednesday	Thursday	Friday	Saturday	Sunday

Notes:

Monthly Planner

Month: ________ **Year:** ________

Monday	Tuesday	Wednesday	Thursday	Friday	Saturday	Sunday

Notes:

Monthly Planner

Month: ________ **Year:** ________

Monday	Tuesday	Wednesday	Thursday	Friday	Saturday	Sunday

Notes:

Monthly Planner

Month: ________ **Year:** ________

Monday	Tuesday	Wednesday	Thursday	Friday	Saturday	Sunday

Notes:

Monthly Planner

Month: ________ **Year:** ________

Monday	Tuesday	Wednesday	Thursday	Friday	Saturday	Sunday

Notes:

Monthly Planner

Month: ________ **Year:** ________

Monday	Tuesday	Wednesday	Thursday	Friday	Saturday	Sunday

Notes:

Monthly Planner

Month: ____________ **Year:** ____________

Monday	Tuesday	Wednesday	Thursday	Friday	Saturday	Sunday
☐	☐	☐	☐	☐	☐	☐
☐	☐	☐	☐	☐	☐	☐
☐	☐	☐	☐	☐	☐	☐
☐	☐	☐	☐	☐	☐	☐
☐	☐	☐	☐	☐	☐	☐

Notes:

Monthly Planner

Month: ________ **Year:** ________

Monday	Tuesday	Wednesday	Thursday	Friday	Saturday	Sunday

Notes:

Monthly Planner

Month: ____________ **Year:** ____________

Monday	Tuesday	Wednesday	Thursday	Friday	Saturday	Sunday

Notes:

Monthly Planner

Month: ________ **Year:** ________

Monday	Tuesday	Wednesday	Thursday	Friday	Saturday	Sunday

Notes:

Made in the USA
Columbia, SC
09 February 2025

53170346R00017